You Are Not Alone

by

Nadja

NadjaMedia.com

NadjaMedia.com

Nadja Media
530 Los Angeles Ave., Suite 115
Moorpark, California 93021

Dedication

To us so we can leave the past behind and grow into the people we were meant to be and take up the Work we were born to do.

Acknowledgments

Thank you to all the people, barring none, that I have had the privilege to be with during my entire life.

Introduction

Do you feel isolated, disconnected, that no one understands? If so this book may help. It is like having an intimate conversation with a friend who truly knows you. It will rekindle hope in those of any age who are distraught to the point of giving up their dreams or even their lives and coax them back into Life to become all they were born to be. Where there is breath there is hope.

Foreword

"Your pain is caused by not knowing
your True Identity." — Prem Rawat

"Know thyself." — Socrates

Dear Friend,

We have not had the pleasure of meeting face-to-face. I would have loved to have found a book like this when I was severely depressed and suicidal. This is my gift to you. May you reap the benefits.

What if thoughts of suicide were really just emergency calls for help? What if they were messages that the way you are thinking your life and living it is definitely not working for you and it is entirely within your power to change it? You think there is no way out, but there is. Always. Yes, your worldview can change. You are not trapped. Your mind does not have to dictate your actions. You are not your thoughts. What if you are just learning some very difficult life lessons? What if life is a school and you are a student here to learn? Do yourself a favor and everyone you know. Take up this challenge before you take your life. This would be an irreversible decision. You are totally capable of change. Give this a chance. This is part of your heritage as a human being. Think of yourself as an explorer rather than a victim. You can do this. The rewards will be way beyond your expectations.

No one is disposable. We are all indispensable – all of us are a piece of the puzzle. We all count – a lot, no matter what. You are absolutely more than you think you are—much more. Reconsider and try another way, seek another viewpoint, heal, and then thrive. You can do this. Yes, you, and someday you will look back upon this period of your life as a time of mistaken identity and you will feel gratitude that you found another way, a different perspective and you discovered and fell in love with your True Self and with life. Take the challenge.

You are worth it. I know. I have been where you are now. I understand. When you want to kill yourself it is the programmed self you want to destroy. It is because you have not yet met your True Self, the part of you that loves you unconditionally, beyond measure, no matter what. It is definitely there and makes all the difference. Wait. Seek within. It's true. Be patient. Never give up. Breathe. Your gifts are waiting to be opened.

If you need assistance check out the resources list at the end of this book. This list is comprised of true way showers and change agents endowed with the spirit of love and compassion. They, too, have overcome tremendous obstacles and are sharing the techniques that have worked for them and have a proven track record in helping others break free.

May you return to balance and stay on the Planet to share your gifts with all of us. You are needed to play an important part during this Time of Great Change and tremendous turbulence. I wish you the very best of all that life has to offer on your journey to find out who you truly are.

In Empathy and Friendship,

Nadja

Contents

Trust

Do you feel,

That no one understands?

No one really hears you?

That they speak

A different language

And you yearn to

Meet *your* people

If they even exist?

Do you feel abandoned

Alone

Left to fend for yourself?

Hello!! Hello??

Is there anyone?

Someone?

Yes, there is

It is your very Soul

That sustains you

And breathes life into you

Perhaps you don't know It

Or feel It

But never fear

It is always with you

It is your closest friend

And companion

Cheering you on

And soothing

Your feathers

Trust

Oh Me, Oh My, Oh Mind

Have you ever felt as brittle

And parched

As a withered leaf

That has been sucked dry

And has fallen to the ground

Eager to return to dust?

Have you ever felt so alone

That there was nothing

And no one

Who could echo back

Or hear your screams

Or your whimpers?

Have you been able to admit this

To someone?

Anyone?

Or even to yourself?

Have you ever felt

So disconnected

So empty

That even if the wind

Toppled you over

No one would ever know

No one would miss you?

Did you ever feel

That your life

With all the struggles

And hardship

Didn't count?

Did you ever feel that you wanted

To curl up into a little ball

And hide yourself

Away from the world forever?

Have you ever felt

So alone

That you think

Even Your Creator has totally

Forgotten your Soul?

Do you want to end it all

To stop the misery?

Well, then, you are not alone.

I have felt this,

And many more

Than we will ever know

Have entertained

These same thoughts

But these are just feelings

And they will not last forever

This, too, shall pass.

It is not the Truth

Of Who You Are

Breathe

Feel your breath

Sit with it

Bathe in it

Know that it is always with you

Breathe

Dry your tears

Connect with your magnificence

Your Soul Song

Your Creator's Love for you

Breathe

Breathe your way back

Into Life

No one is suffocating you but you

Breathe

You are too precious

To spcnd your time like this

You are too valuable

To waste one minute

Breathe

In spite of appearances

All is well and you are loved

Loved beyond all measure

No matter what

Breathe

Feel life coming in

To say, "Hello."

Breathe

Keep breathing

Hug yourself

Wake up

Snap out of it

Greet the day

And take it on!

Hey, you bought

A round-trip ticket

From Heaven to Earth

No fair going back

Before schedule

Best to get your money's worth

Breathe

Relax

Breathe

Relax

I love you

Breathe

Homework

Are you ready to release

To let go

To surrender?

Your life is waiting

Untouchable

Did you learn the art

Of crying on the inside

And smiling on the outside

While you slowly froze

All of your feelings

One by one

Until

At long last

Nothing bothered you

And nothing touched you

You were pain free

And totally disconnected

From everyone

But most importantly

From

You

Lot's Wife

The wife of Lot

Looked back to see

What she did

In her history

When she focused

On the past

Emotions flooded in

The spell was cast

Was it her fault

That she turned to salt

Frozen in a pillar

No humanity in her?

Her heart became stone

She was totally alone

Is there hope for her?

Can she return to life?

Or will she forever

Be the stone-hearted wife?

After years as a pillar

The nourishing rain came

The salt melted

And Lot's wife changed

She learned her lesson

After being frozen alone

Her heart melted

And no longer was stone

She welcomed life

Abundance and laughter

She became human

And a loving benefactor

She now could relate

To the human race

Her former life

Left absolutely no trace

Returning fully to Life

Embracing it all

As a Child of Grace

After being frozen in fear

For too many a year

She now has the tools

To help others clear

Welcome Home

Our outer personage

Is built up like scaffolding

From experiences and programming

And then clothed, quaffed, and made up

Until the end result

Is who we think we are

But scaffolding can collapse

And

The carefully constructed ego

Can disintegrate...

Underneath it all

You discover a Gift

A Treasure

Your True Heart

Which beats

In rhythm

With the Source

Of All that Is

Birthday

Who are you

Hiding behind your mask?

Do you even know?

I would love to be with you

When you find out

In fact, I cannot help but

Be with you,

On that eventful day

For we are all One

Abusers

Abusers have no clue

Of how they charge

Into others' lives

And crash into their Hearts

To create havoc

They have no boundaries

They trample on people

In a fit of anger or madness

That they have not processed

And therefore need people

To stick it all on

To vomit it out on

To feel they have power over

Because they do not have control

Over themselves

Or their lives

They are clueless

Lost

They need us to set boundaries

So they can become conscious

Of what they are doing

Of what they are saying

So they, too, can heal

And no longer be

A destructive force

In our world

They, too,

Act out of their experiences

And mistaken identities

They need our help

To stop them

To make them aware

Of what they do

What happened to *them*

That they cannot recognize

What they are doing

And the abuse they spew out

Into the world?

They must feel

Very small

Indeed

That they have to inflict pain

On others

To feel that they

Are even

Alive

We Are All One

So much in this world

Is determined by

What birth canal

We choose

To incarnate through

Saying, "No"

How does it feel

When you can't

Say the word, "No"

You can form the letters

With your mouth and lips

But your voice

Will not give sound to it

It becomes stuck

In your throat

And in your heart

And takes up space

In every cell

For decades

Or a lifetime

Is this from years

Of child abuse

When saying "no"

Was strictly forbidden

And severely punished

When you felt you had

Absolutely no rights

To protect yourself

And you were the property

Of those who had the right

To do anything they wished to you

And you were too small

To fight them off

Your feelings didn't count to them

You were not important enough

To be consulted about

How *you* felt

And what *you*

Thought about things

You were an object

For others to act upon

And you didn't

Feel worthy enough

To say anything about your pain

Or perhaps

You hadn't even learned

How to talk yet

Yes

These things take over our words

Our hearts, our minds, our life

Until we finally realize

We are a Child of a Loving Creator

Who wants the very best for us

And that we can heal

We can totally clear

We can speak out

For our protection

And the protection of others

We do not have to accept abuse

In a world

That looks the other way

When bullies do their thing

Yes

We have permission

To say the words

"No"

"Stop"

"I don't like what you are doing."

And hang up the phone

Leave

Shut the door

And congratulate ourselves

On breaking

The long,

Difficult

Spell

Of

Silence

Of we are not enough

Of we are not worthy

Of speaking up

All that is required of these words

Is that we say them with our

Full Power

We do not have to scream or yell

The words can come out quietly

But they come out

With full strength

Behind them

And people hear them

Really hear them

With their ears

With their hearts

With their minds

Onward Toward Victory

Is it fair for us

To give other people

So much power over us

That our lives

And our memories

Are in their hands?

So much power

That we are making them

Our jailers

Our prison guards

Could we be creating monsters?

Are we the problem?

We are definitely part

Of the problem

And we must be responsible

For cleaning up our own cesspool

So others don't feel

Like they can dump *their* waste

Into it as well

We must be brave enough

To step fully into life

To face our fears

Our destructive habits

To face as well

Our strengths and our power

To create healthy boundaries

So others cannot

Come crashing through

We are walking through centuries

Of oppression and suppression

To claim our Victory

As Whole Human Beings

Who know how to love

No matter what

And know how to melt hearts

That have turned to stone

Starting

With

Our own

Gifts of Grace

I look forward to the day

When your scorpion sting

Enters my energy field

And does not rattle a thing

Up until now I have allowed it in

To pierce me through

And put me in a jagged state

Where I am completely lost

And know not what to do

However,

After straightening out

My feathers

I take your sting

As a Gift of Grace

That shows me

The places inside of me

Which only I can erase

Reacting vs. Responding

A tone of voice

A look

A comment

Misinterpreted

And twisted by

False assumptions

When processed

Through the filter

Of life experiences

Can change

Your emotional climate

From sunny skies

To thunder storms

In one nano-second

Causing you to react

To hang up the phone

To slam the door

To shut your heart

And guillotine a relationship

Sending it into oblivion

Forever

Cheating yourself

Out of the possibility

Of self-liberation

By breathing through it

Welcoming neutrality

And seeing it for what it is

Even

From

The *other* person's perspective

Then responding (not re-acting)

With a balanced,

Calm

Heart-centered

Presence

An Event Is

An event is an event

No matter what happened

Or how it went

We color it with

What we think

And how we feel

It then becomes part of

Our onion peel

The goal is to experience

With neutrality

So we can fully merge

With Totality

And empty our cells

Of all the dross

That our thinking and feelings

Have caused at great cost

Discipline

Stop before you react

Take a breath before you reply

Try to see it differently

Through the *other* person's eye

Giving Your Power Away

Have you ever been so distraught

That you allowed your life

To hang in the hands

Of a waitress

Who smiled at you

And said, ''How are you today?''

And really meant it?

Of a dog

Who came up to you

Wagging its tail and

Wanting you to pet it?

Of a stranger

Who smiled

And nodded "Hello" to you

On the street?

How frail and fragile

Our egos are

When they are disconnected

From our Soul

From Source.

Our drug of choice

Even if it is shopping

Or eating

Only numbs us

And keeps us from

Totally participating

In our experiences.

Even so

Until we learn to let go

And trust

We may have to come back

Again and again

To revisit

Our challenges

Until at last

We learn

That

Love

Is

Always

The

Answer.

You Are Enough

Have you ever been so terrified

That you were afraid

To walk out of

Your front door

Thinking you were

Scared of meeting people

But truly you were frightened

Because you had no clue as to

Who *you* were?

Even though people told you

Their version

Of who you were

You knew you weren't that

Yet you said nothing

For you didn't know

Your own Being

You couldn't find your stability

Your core

Your center of gravity

It was so easy

For others

To throw you off balance

With a word, a look,

A tone of voice

And you hadn't learned how

To create a false front

A defense system

With which to interface

With the world

A *personality*, they call it

Have you ever strategized

When and how to leave a location

In order to avoid

Seeing certain people?

Have you ever laid yourself down

In a field of tall grass

In order not to be seen at all?

Were you caught

Between the worlds

Of Here and The Far Country

One foot in each world

At the same time?

Do you have trouble deciding which one

To place both feet in?

When people talked with you

Did you wonder

Who they thought

They were talking to?

Did you feel so disconnected

That your only choice was

To hide behind pretend feelings

And pretend words

Which made you feel

Even more disconnected?

Was everyone pretending

And you were the only one

Aware of it?

Were you awake while dreaming?

Was everyone acting

And lying to themselves

And not wanting to see?

Or maybe they just

Didn't know

Weren't aware

Not recognizing they are

On the World Stage

As an actor

(Not who they truly are)

In the Drama of Life

If so

Welcome to the

Grand Masquerade Party

Come with me

You are enough

No need to practice your script

You may be silent

If you so choose

Just observe

Accept my invitation

I will be your chaperon

For I have walked this trail

For many, many years

And now

I can

Guide you

To

Your

Self

Instill Wholeness

Hello out there

How do you do?

I'll let you See me

Will you let me See You?

Empaths

When you're in a room with people

Do you sop up their emotions

Like people used to do

With bread and gravy

Savoring every drop, every morsel

Have you quit reading novels

Because you step into the pages

And become the characters

And live their lives

When you go to the movies

Do they become your life

And your experience forever

Are there any boundaries

Like where you stop

And they begin

When you go to the mall

Do you come home exhausted

Not from shopping

But from collecting

The emotions and problems

Of all the busy shoppers

Who are afraid to be alone

With their own thoughts

Especially now

As the disintegration

Of the third dimension

Has stepped up its frenetic tempo

Tremendously

Can you feel a tree

Being chopped down

And hear its cries

What do you do

When you sense people's motives

Before they speak

Even though *they* have no clue

How do you handle people

Feeding off your energy

How is it for you

When a person

Attacks you

With their viperous tongue

And then they walk away

Relieved

And you walk away

With their poisonous arrows

Stuck in your body

Draining away the pus

For hours, days, years, decades

Perhaps a lifetime, or longer

How does all that feel to you?

Sensitivity is a two-edged sword

It can be a curse

Or a blessing

It must be handled with care

And with Knowledge

Otherwise it can cripple you

And eventually destroy you

Until you learn how to

Wield its power

And see the Gift in it

So that you can observe a flower

And feel yourself growing leaves

And welcoming

The array of insects

To pollinate you

You feel the joy

Of radiating its beauty

Into the world

And the ability to breathe forth

Its delicious aroma

You can actually

Catch a ride on a butterfly

And experience

The freedom

And exuberance it feels

Having been

Released from its cocoon

You can walk on the beach

And ride the waves

To a distant shore

Without a surfboard

Or a boat

Yes

The Native Americans say

All our Relations

Perhaps it is just All

Like All One

Or just

ONE

How is it for you?

Do you know

What I am talking about?

Have you experienced this

And lived it?

Then

Welcome

You are an empath

Welcome, My Friend,

You are not alone

And you will grow to appreciate

Your sensitivity

Your Gift

As you cover this world

With your Love

And plant

Daffodils

Choices

I have run from human love

For as long as I can remember

I chose to sequester myself

Until the last dying ember

I admit this is the coward's way

To protect the fragile ego

Rather than to live from the heart

And just let it all release and flow

Mother Nature speaks to me

From the depths of her very Being

It's the only place on Earth

Where I feel free to Be and be seen

Permission to Talk

Isn't it interesting

That when you are silent

People assume

You have nothing to say

Little do they know

You are waiting for permission

To speak

One Hand Clapping

I have always felt

Like one hand clapping

For as long as I can remember

But I just realized

My one hand met

The Hand of the Universe

I was not alone after all

I was participating all the while

Cosmically connected

Whether one hand or two

We clap

As one

Alone

A lone

Al One

All One

Let's Be Real

How does it feel

To be awake in a World

Where most are sleepwalking?

What is there to say

When all the talk is about

Gossip, weather, TV, politics, religion, food?

Why isn't there

Something of importance

To be discussed

Like

How does your heart feel

As they rip out the guts

Of our Mother Earth?

Do you feel like crying

As they poison the skies

And our oceans

With their ignorant blindness

And their brave new technologies?

What does it bring up for you

When you see humans trample on

The rights of others,

Take away their livelihood,

Their health,

Destroy their land,

Their homes,

Their lives

And cause them

To turn to dust?

Did it affect you

To see the saffron-robed monks

Incinerate themselves

To protest the inhumanity

In their corner of the Earth?

Did you change the channel

Or reach for another bucket

Of Colonel Sanders

Or both?

What about

The bees?

Does anyone know?

Does anyone care?

Does anyone give a crap

That humanity is destroying itself

By quickly dismantling

The Web of Life?

Wake up!

Noah's Ark

Is parked

Outside our Door

Full of Oneself

I am in the grasp of

Overwhelming sadness

As I start this day

I am caught in a trap

Of my own making

There is enough sadness

And tragedy in this world

To fill it full

Why add to this energy

When I know better

It is not the world's sadness

But only my own

Compounded by the selfishness

Of it all

I feel I am about to drown

———————

Stand tall

Reach down

And open your heart

Forgive yourself

And forgive all

There are those

Who hear your call

Enough Already!!

How could we have

Remained silent

After years of seeing pictures

Of starving children

Emaciated people

Behind the barbed wire fences

Of concentration camps

People being beheaded

Women stoned to death in amphitheaters

Taking the rap for their husbands'

Sexual addictions

Leaders of many religions

Twisting scripture into

Platforms of hatred and division

Mothers killing their children

Innocent people being incarcerated,

Tortured,

Executed

Girls being kidnapped

And sold as sex slaves

Babies thrown alive

Into dumpsters

Or flushed down toilets

Single parents

Raising their kids in cars

Homeless people begging for food

The Military Industrial Complex

Killing, raping,

Plundering, and pillaging

All over the Globe

The elderly dying in ''homes''

That are just holding tanks

Animals being gassed

By the thousands

In ''shelters''

Children abused

And used for pornography films

Kids killing their parents

People of all ages

Who can't afford medical care

Or whose insurance companies

Refuse to take action

Dying painful deaths at home

Women, mothers, and grandmothers,

Divorced and

Thrown out of their homes

Penniless

Because they no longer

Share the bed

With their former husbands

Soldiers

Who come home from battle

Scarred, disabled, and mentally ill

Disregarded and

Turned out on the streets

To fend for themselves

Latch key children

Hiding behind doors

Alcoholic men beating their wives

And children into submission

Violence and gun shots

In our cities

Politicians grabbing

What they can get away with

Neighbors being dragged

Against their will

Out of their own homes

That have been foreclosed on

By the banks

Where is our humanity

Where has it gone

What is happening

The madness is

Overwhelming!

Insanity and ignorance

Are running rampant

All over our Planet

However

In spite of all that

There are those of courage

Who have not given up

Who still hold the Light

And keep

The flames of Truth burning

To herald a New Day

When all the chaos

Will be stilled

And Peace will reign

Truth

Below the surface

Truth eagerly awaits

Our discovery

Blast Off

Tears caught in the heart

Created by sadness and fears

Stuck in the throat

Creating a moat

Between my

Inner and Outer worlds

To cross this moat

Is a treacherous ride

For that is where the ego and Higher Self

Hang out and hide

To blast through this

Will take a nuclear force

Equal to every cell in my body

Blasting off

All right

If that's what it takes

Let's go

I have had all

That I can humanly take

From my fully entrenched

Imperfectly programmed ego

Cultural Conditioning

Do not let the Collective Mind

Limit and define

Step outside the boundaries

Join the adventuresome few

Become all of who you are

Create yourself new

Conversation with Spirit

You are just starting

To know what love is

To welcome Source

To pour Itself

Into your body

And fill each cell

And merge with you

In a most gentle way

Without words

So you can sense It

So you don't bolt

Or erect barriers in a nano-second

Because change is so frightening

So you can feel It

And allow It to grow you

Past all of your resistance

Your filters

So you can allow It

To melt your heart

And your ego

Into

Warm

Golden

Honey

Stepping Out

Have I finally

Written all the words out

Have I emptied

On the cellular level

All the accumulated dross

From more years

Than I care to count

Have I cleansed this

From all my systems

And lifetimes

Forever

Have I said

What needed to be said

To clear myself

To move on

And help others

Begin their process

And clear

Can I now

Be the woman

I was meant to be

Before I took birth

Do I dare

Give myself permission

To be fully who I am

To step onto

The World Stage

As myself

Just me

Is that all that's required of me

Just to be me

Really

Is that all

That's so easy

Now that I know how

To drop all the rest

I am crying tears of relief

I can feel

I can open

And do not have to close anymore

I can release the past

And

Trust

As I step into

My Truth

My Birthright

My Abundance

And

My

Most

Succulent

Life

Wondrous Woman

Life lived

Heart bared

Beauty hid

Running scared

Personal demons

Chasing you

What can you

Possibly do

Try to confront them

This doesn't work

Befriend and disarm them

Meanwhile don't shirk

Your many duties in this life

Filled with hardship

Filled with strife

All that tension

All that stress

Comes to naught

When you confess

Your part in the drama

That created the mess

At last you can stand

At last you can see

To finally be able

To let it all Be

Just relax and be you

Underneath it all

Breathe deeply

Stand tall

Able to love

Not in spite of

But because of it all

Freedom

I put myself in jail

And threw away the key

Then late in life

I found it again

And set myself free

It's wonderful to wake each day

And ask Source to guide my way

To welcome in the morning sun

Be creative and have fun

Filled with gratitude

When day is done

There's nothing like a Free Soul

And loving yourself

Back to Whole

Insight

I was lonely

And in ill health

Until I met my

Inner Self

What a surprise

To know that I

Had treasures within

Great Inner Wealth

That carried me through

The thick and the thin

And was more of a companion

And comforter to me

Than anyone else

Could have ever been

It gave me great stability

Taught me how

To really See

And best of all

Just how to Be

No pressure on me

To figure it out

Or to be more

The whole purpose was

To relax

And restore

See the world

With New Eyes

Understand its perfection

And quietly

Just

Self-Realize

Re-Inventing Yourself

What's amazing

In this life

Is that we can

Re-create ourselves

Into anything we please

Especially now

Best to use the building blocks

Of gratitude, kindness, and love

And let all the rest go

Then surrender

And let Source

Grow you

Into

Your

Full

Stature

Keep A - Goin,' Sister

Keep a-goin,' Sister

Keep a dancin'

Keep a knowin,' Sister

Keep advancin'

It ain't gonna get better, Sister

But you certainly will

Keep a growin,' Sister

Keep practicin' bein' still

A balanced love warrior

Walkin' on the Earth

Strong as Iron

Led by the heart

And awakened self-worth

Soon you can greet the world

With eyes wide open

Accept it how it is

No dreamin' no hopin'

We see you, Sister

From the other side

So proud of you

Nothing left to hide

Keep a-goin,' Sister

Walkin' in the Light

No more judgin,' Sister

No more wrong or right

Keep a-goin,' Sister

Keep a glowin'

Keep a dancin,' Sister

Keep a knowin'

It ain't gonna get better, Sister

But you certainly will

Keep a growin,' Sister

Keep practicin' bein' still

Self-Care

Above All

Forgive yourself

Be kind to yourself

Honor yourself

For you

Are a child

Of the Most High

And

Are

Precious

And

Deserving

Of

Your

Complete

And

Full

Awakening

Requiem

Our lives are

A sacred journey

No matter how

We choose to live them out

Best to be lived

As conscious, aware Beings

So we can savor each moment

And knowingly

Connect

With All That Is

And

Especially

Joy

Helpful Exercise

The author found that the following exercise helped free her from looking for love and approval outside herself. This was created by Al Diaz, International Keynote Speaker, Author, and Film Producer. He suggests that you do this daily for a month or longer. Check with your doctor before doing this exercise. This is not a substitute for medical advice.

Stand in front of a mirror and look deeply into the pupil of your left eye and say these words slowly with deep feeling, "(Your Name), I fully accept and honor all of who and what you are and I love you unconditionally." Repeat this by looking into the pupil of your right eye. End with repeating again with the pupil of your left eye.

Final Words

"What lies behind us and what lies before us are

tiny matters compared to what lies within us."

— Ralph Waldo Emerson

Resources

HelpGuide.org — Free resources to help you resolve mental and emotional health issues. Includes hotlines and support groups. Helps you help yourself and others.

Children of Domestic Violence (cdv.org)

The Complete Empath Toolkit
by Michael R. Smith

The Emotion Code by Bradley Nelson

Emotional Freedom Technique (EFT)

Matt Kahn

Tarek Bibi

Christine Day

Sophia Zoe

Andie DePass

Chief Golden Light Eagle

Janet Doerr

Karen LaGrange

Jean Houston

Jeff Gignac

Emmanuel Dagher

Tamra Oviatt

isands.org

MagentaPixie.com

HealthBeyondBelief.com

FoodBabe.com

Mercola.com

ScottWerner.org

NaturalNews.com

Bioneers.org

WestonPrice.org

NextWorldTV.com

Cohousing.org

Findhorn.org

PattyGreer.com

Crimes Against Nature
by Robert F. Kennedy

Cosmic Ordering Made Easier
by Ellen Watts

M. T. Keshe

Santos Bonacci

Dr. Masaru Emoto

Vandana Shiva

Masanobu Fukuoka

Chunyi Lin

Susun Weed

Tusli Gabbard

Paul Stamets

Buckmaster Fuller

David Wilcock

Lynn Waldrop

Christel Hughes

Debora Wayne

Lanna Spencer

John Hagelin, Ph.D

Jo Dunning

Lisa Transcendence Brown

Julie Renee

Eckhart Tolle

Neale Donald Walsch

Dorian Light

Lottie Cooper

Judy Cali

Marianne Williamson

Dr. Madlena Kantscheff

Dipal Shah

Peta Amber Lynn

Jarrad Hewett

Cathy Hohmeyer

Morry Zelcovitch

SARK

Shiloh Sophia

Aviva Gold

Ho'oponopono

Acim.org

Wopg.org

BirthingAndRebirthing.com

Chanchka.com

CalixtoSuarez.com

RingingCedars.com

YouWealthRevolution.com

FromHeartacheToJoy.com

AcousticHealth.com

GalacticConnection.com

ByDivineGrace.com

NotesFromTheUniverse.com

TED Talks

Homeopathic Cell Salts

OptimumHealthInstitute.com

NewPhoenixRising.com

About The Author

After working many years in the public sector Nadja is reinventing herself as an artist and writer. She has an eclectic background. Her joys include adventuring on the Open Road, dancing, cooking, being in nature, writing and painting. She is also interested in natural building, organic gardening, alternative health, life-long learning, travel, and living moment to moment. Nadja writes for the conscious community and people who are interested in healing, meditation, transformation, ascension, and the New Earth. This includes highly sensitive people, Starseeds, Indigos, empaths, Light Workers, energy healers, artists, visionaries, and those in recovery and discovery.

Also By Nadja

Soft-cover books, eBooks, MP3s, and CDs,
Smashwords, Amazon, Kindle, CreateSpace,
CDBaby, iTunes, YouTube, and your local
bookstore by request.

River of Living Light

Evolution Revolution

Random Thoughts and Poems

Hopi Blue Corn

El Maiz Azul de los Hopis

Visionary Tales for the New Earth

Color Me Bright Coloring Book

Blue Sky

Ascension Codes

Raps, Chants, and Rants

Women's Power Awakened

Ozzengoggle Poems

From the City of Shem

You Are Not Alone

Family Secrets

Flying Heart

Bullies

www.ingramcontent.com/pod-product-compliance
Lightning Source LLC
Chambersburg PA
CBHW070812050426
42452CB00011B/1999